Whoops Divers Guide Enhanced

MIKE HUGHES

Copyright © 1999 Mike Hughes

All rights reserved.

ISBN: 0-9664130-2-4

Other Books by Mike Hughes:

The Northwest Dive Guide
Harbour Publishing Copyright 2009

The North American Dive Guide
Copyright 2012

Best Of Intentions
Copyright 2012

To Kill A Diver
Copyright 1998 Printed 2013

Whoops Airlines Enhanced
Copyright 1998 Printed 2014

DEDICATION
This book is dedicated to Ron Akeson

ALL SPELLING ERRORS ARE INTENTIONALLY DONE ON PORPOISE TO REFLECT THE COLLOQUIAL SPEECH PATTERNS OF LIVE HUMANS.

Some errors were done just for the Halibut.

WHOOPS AIRLINES

OLD BOTTLE COLLECTING

I TOLD YOU NOT TO KEEP YOUR SPEAR GUN LOADED.

WHOOPS AIRLINES

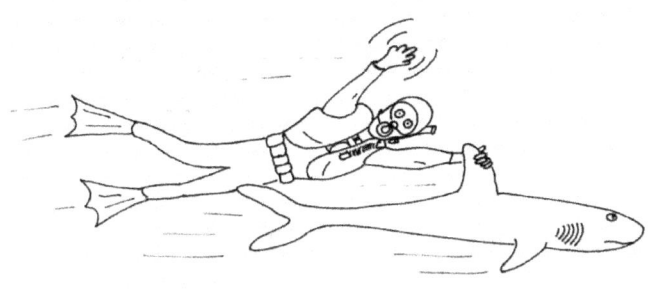

THE ADVANCED DIVER

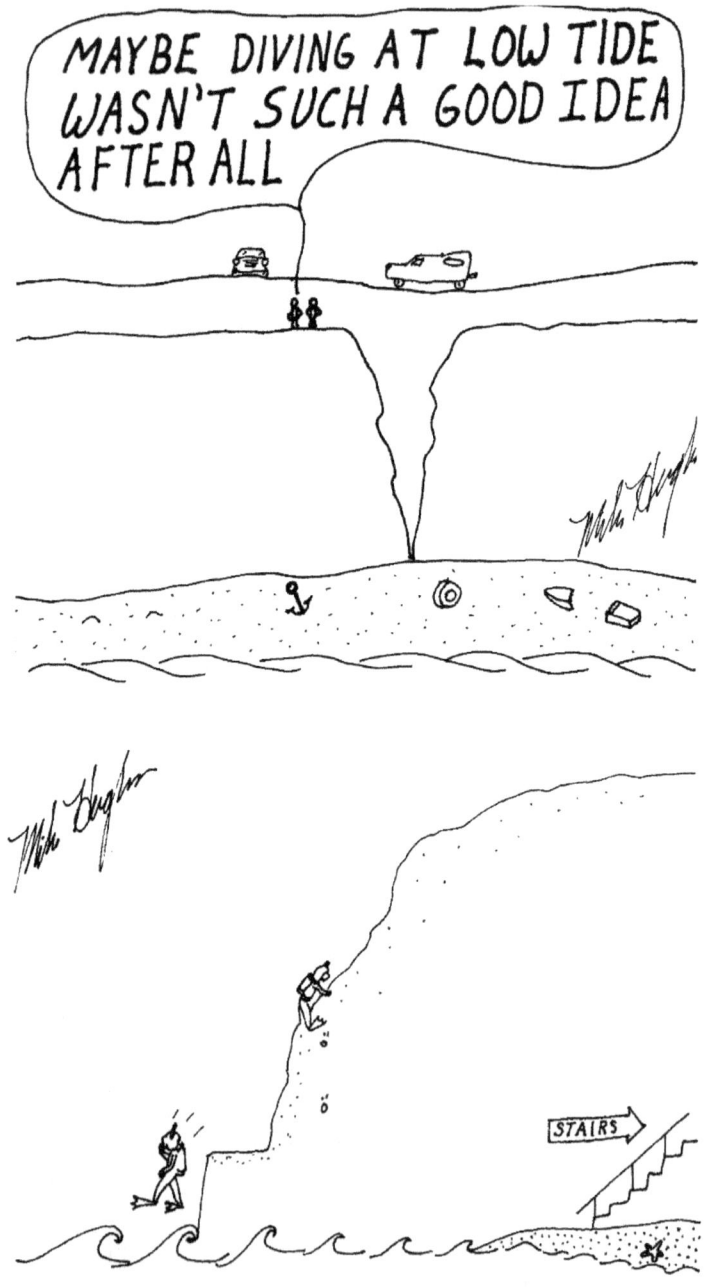

HARLEY DIVESON

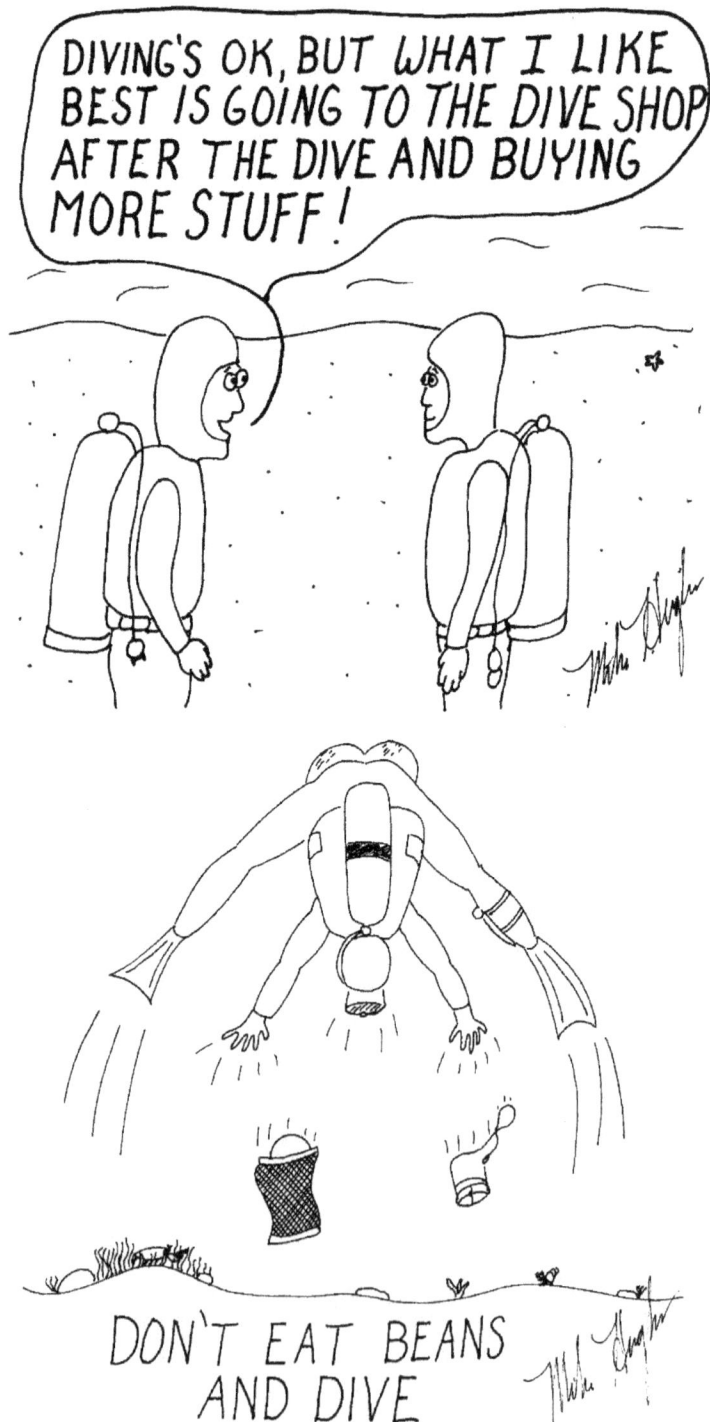

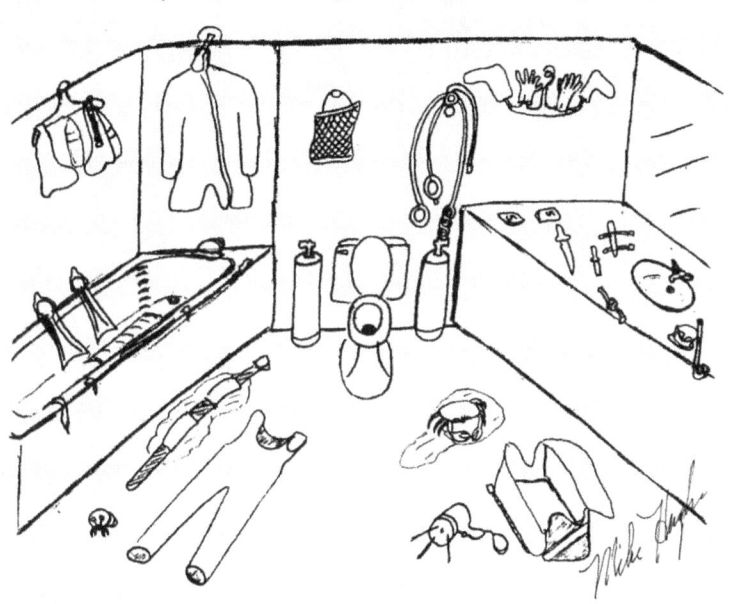

WHOOPS AIRLINES

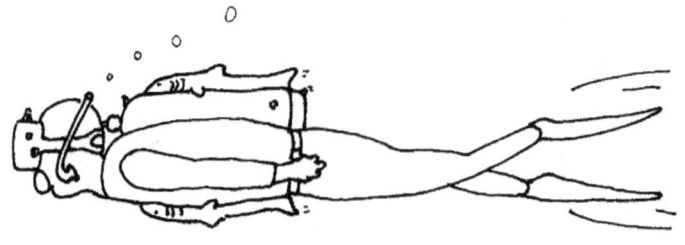

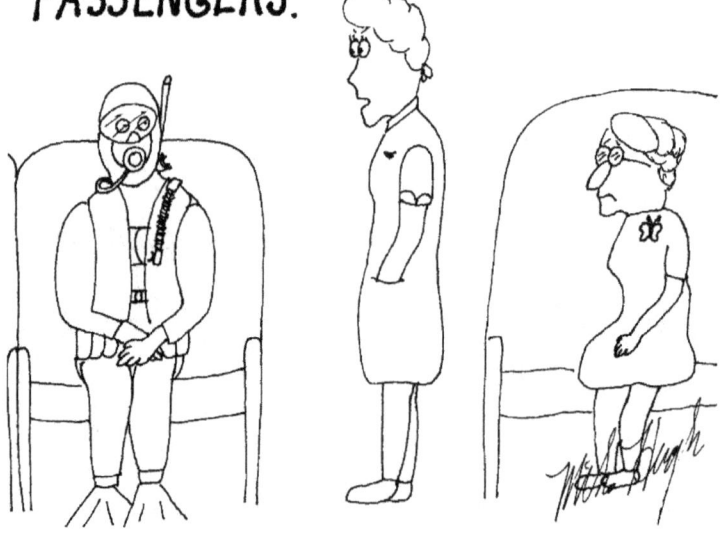

WHOOPS AIRLINES

UDDER WATER DIVING

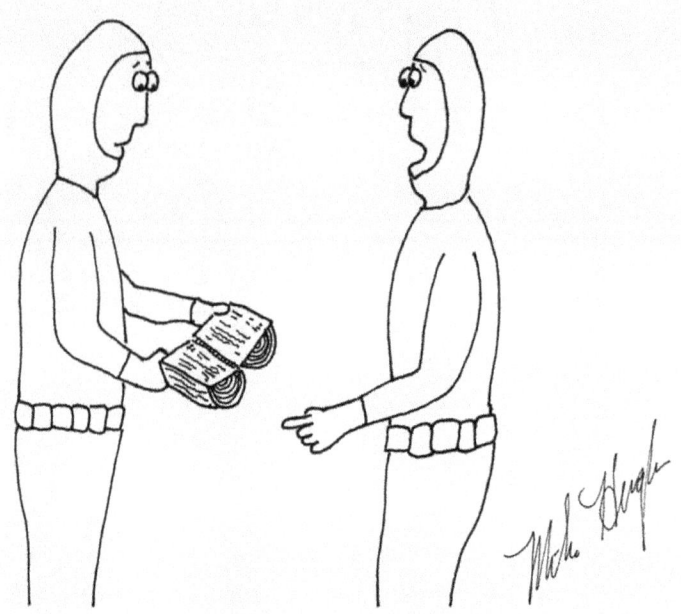

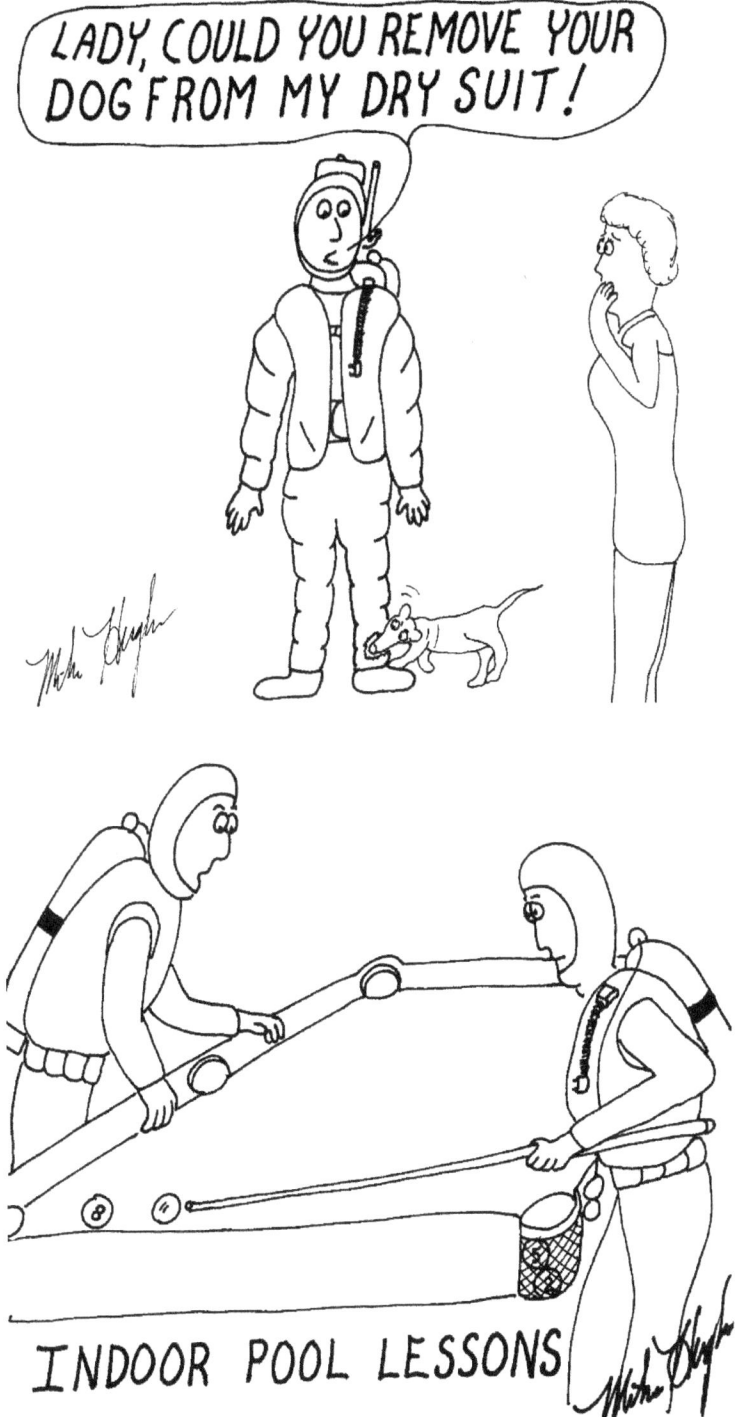

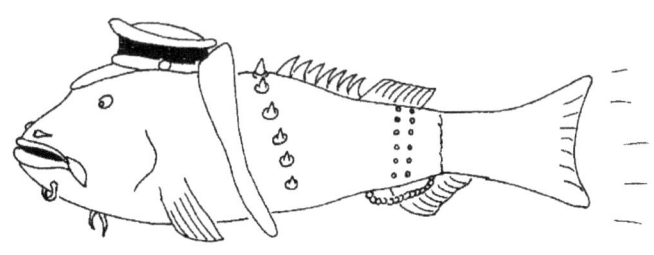

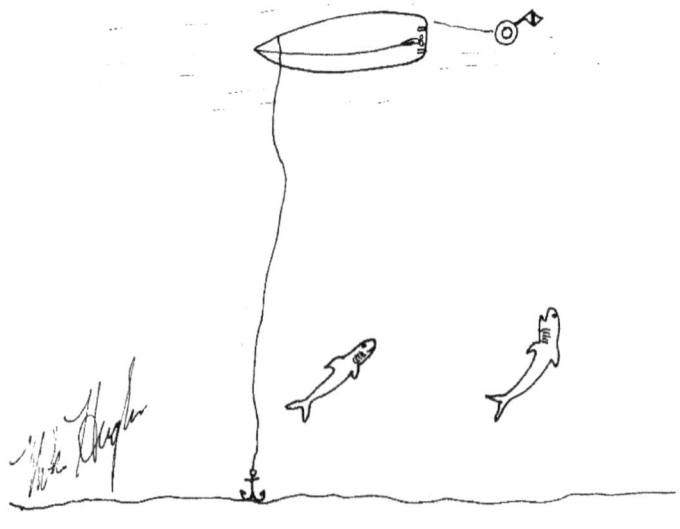

THE REASON FOR DIVE TABLES

THE ABYSMAL NIGHT DIVE

WHOOPS AIRLINES

THE PRACTICAL JOKER

WHOOPS AIRLINES

THE JOY OF EXITING SHORE DIVES

ARTIFICIAL REEF PROJECTS

PRIVATELY FUNDED $10,000

GOVERNMENT COST 5 TRILLION

SO MUCH FOR USING A DIVE FLAG

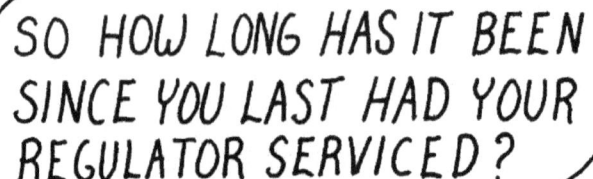

SIR, AS A GAME WARDEN, I'D LIKE TO REMIND YOU THAT YOU CAN'T REMOVE ANY WILD LIFE FROM THIS AREA.

WHEN CUTTING YOUR BUDDY'S FINGER COULD SAVE YOUR LIFE.

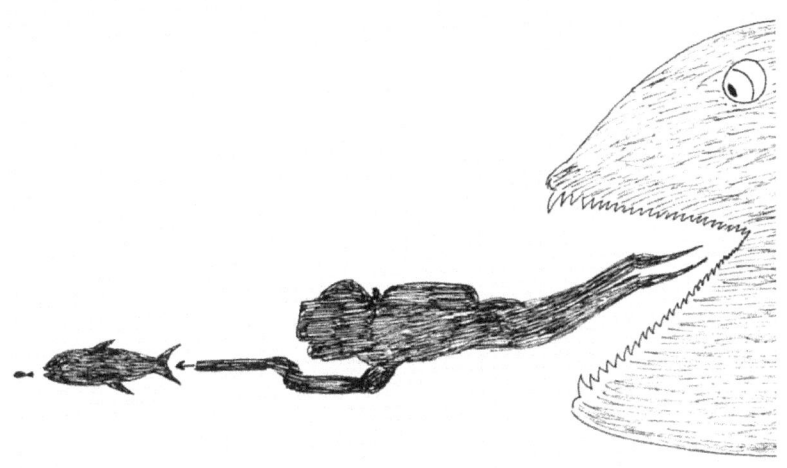

THE NIGHT DIVER

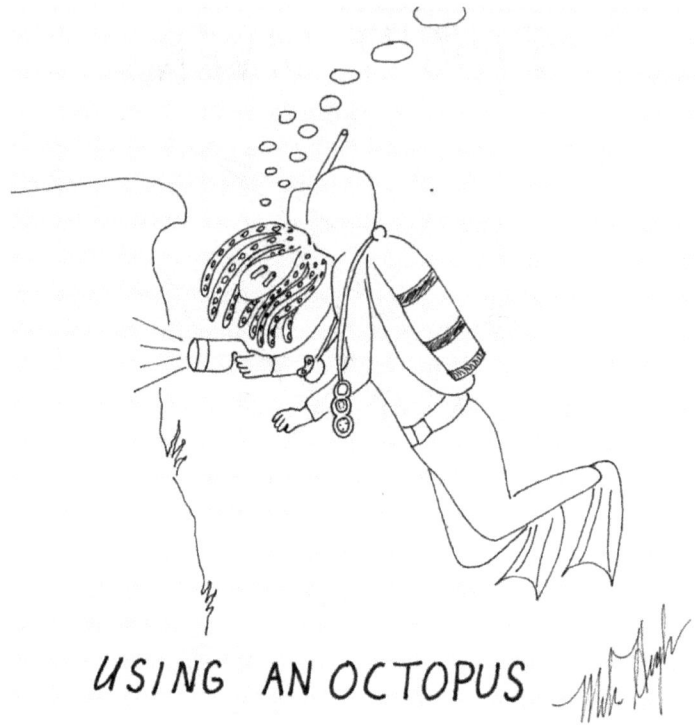

USING AN OCTOPUS

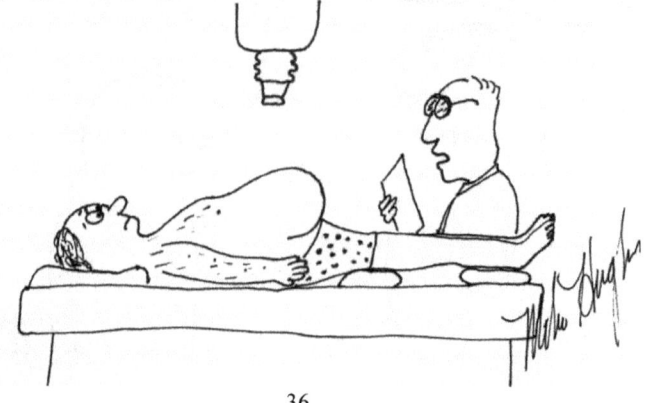

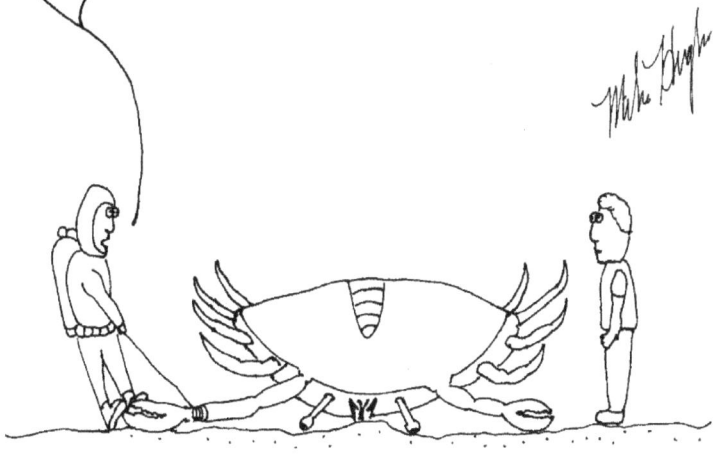

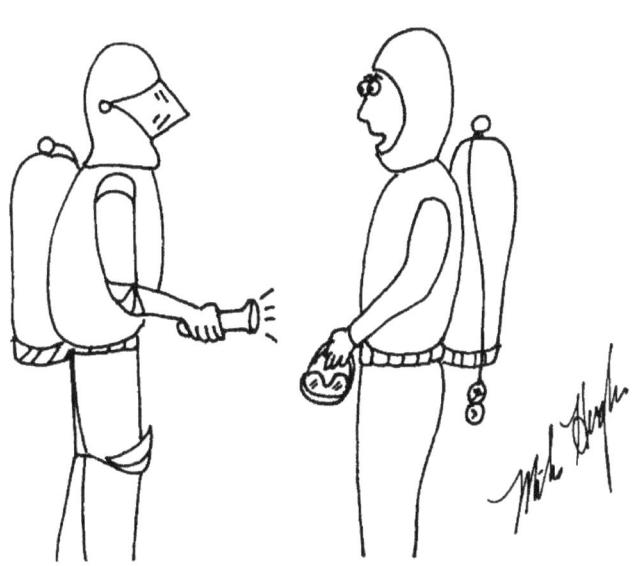

Never confuse NITROX (enriched air) with NITROUS OXIDE (laughing gas).

WHOOPS AIRLINES

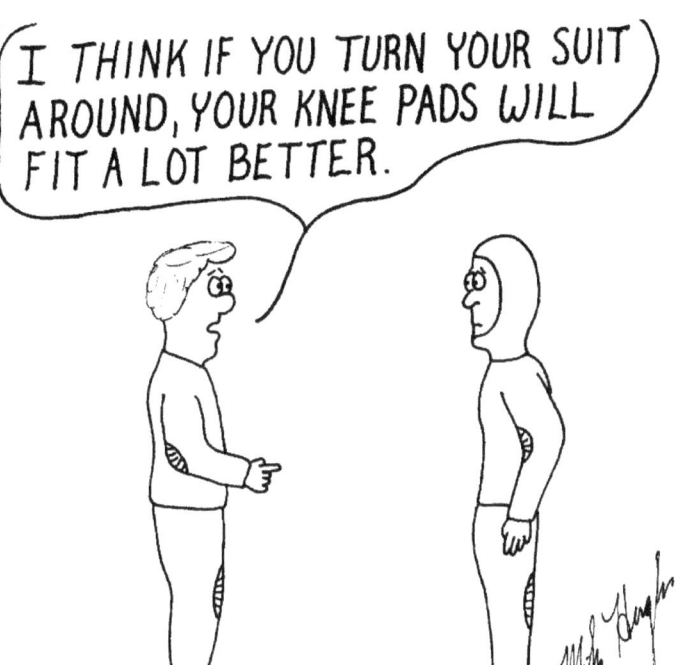

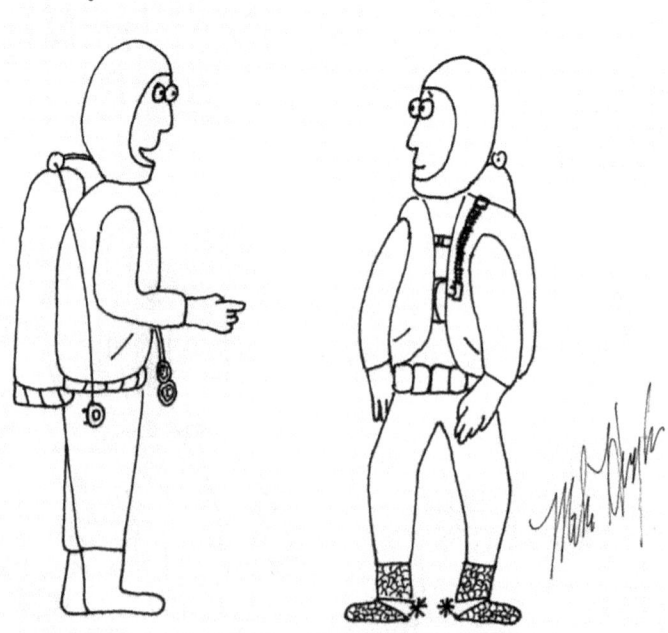

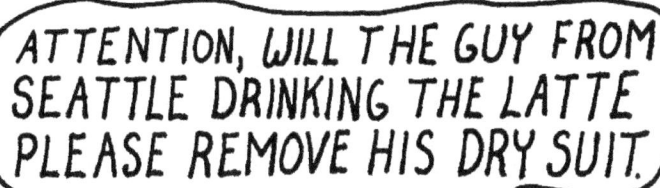

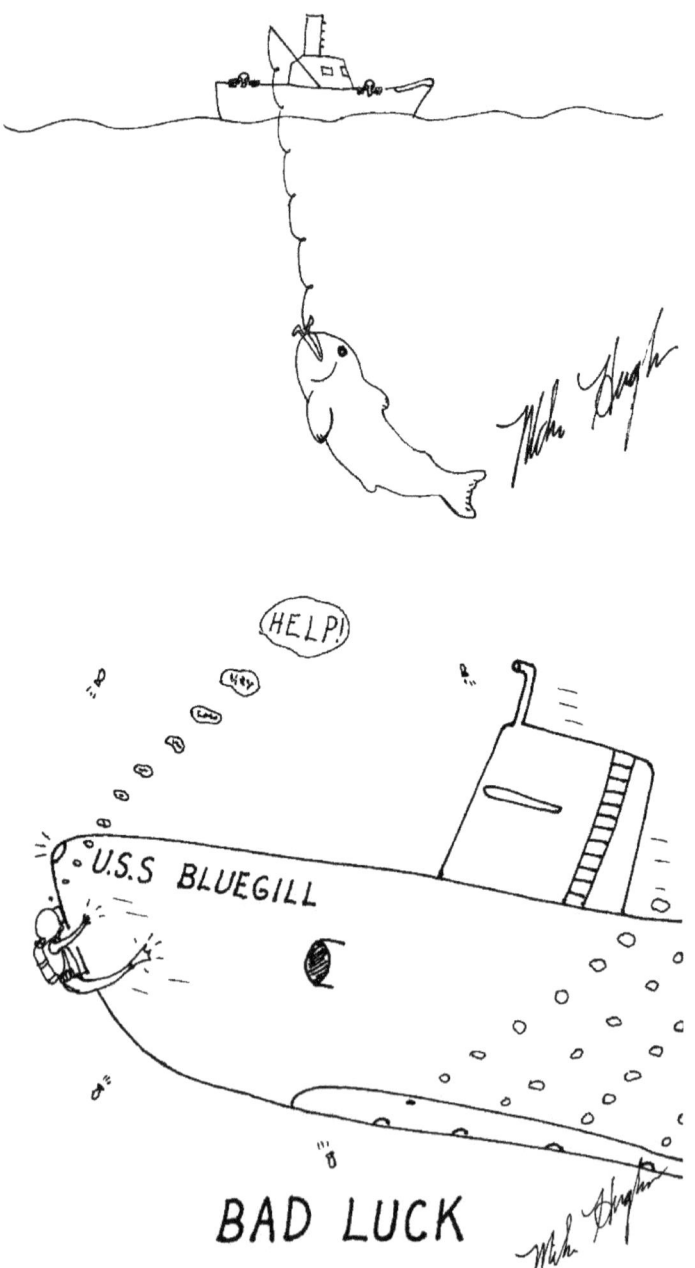

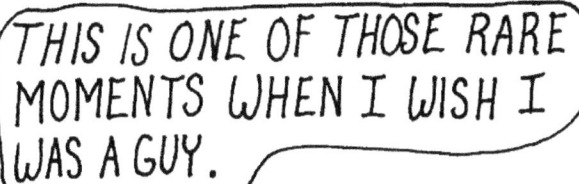

SYMBIOTIC RELATIONSHIPS

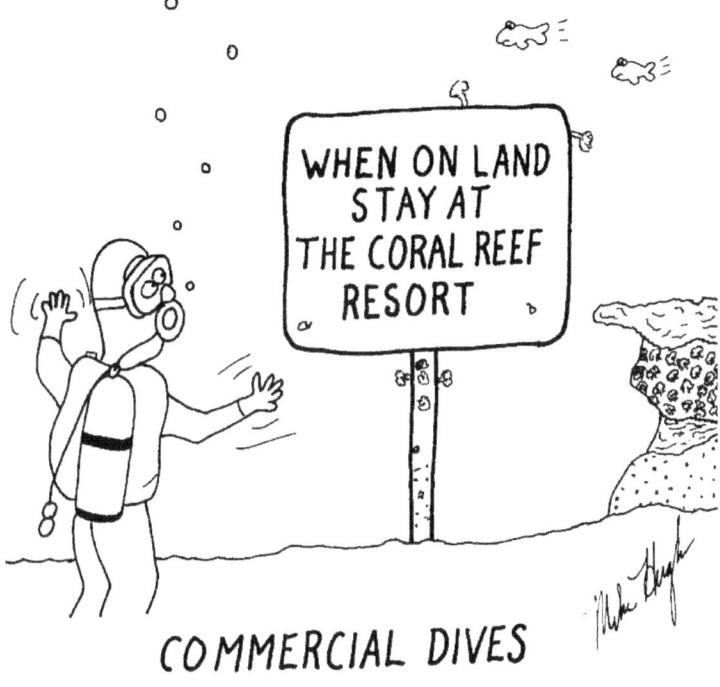

COMMERCIAL DIVES

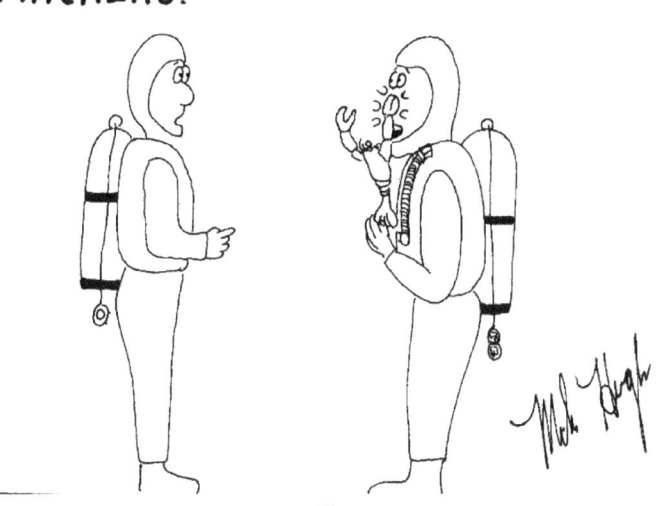

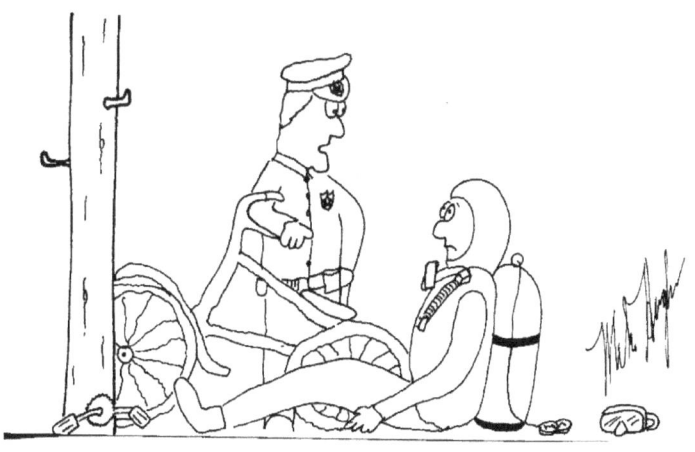
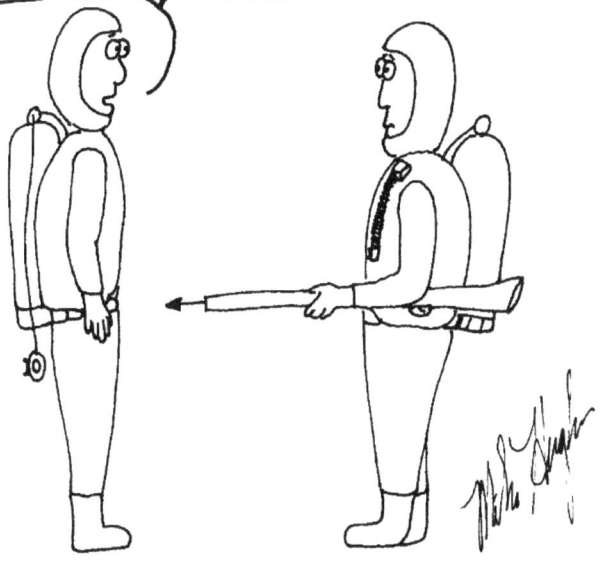

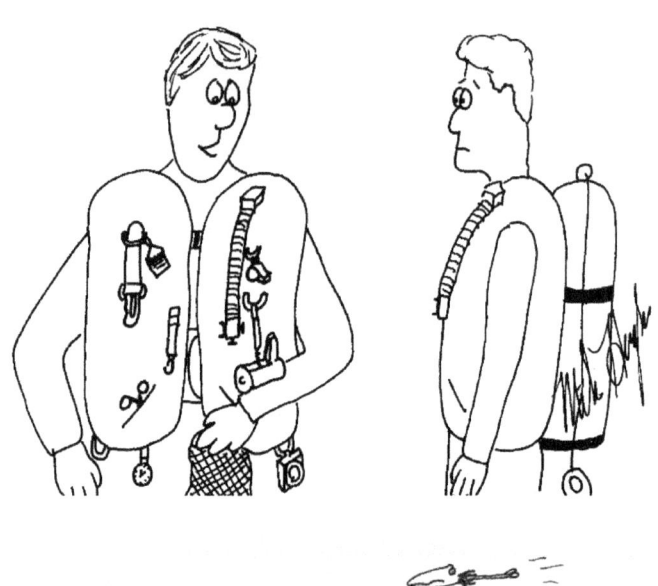

SHELL COLLECTING

EARLY DIVE COMPUTERS

BEWARE THE EEL TEASERS

THE GREAT FLOOD

RECOGNIZING SIGNS OF TERRITORIAL SHARKS

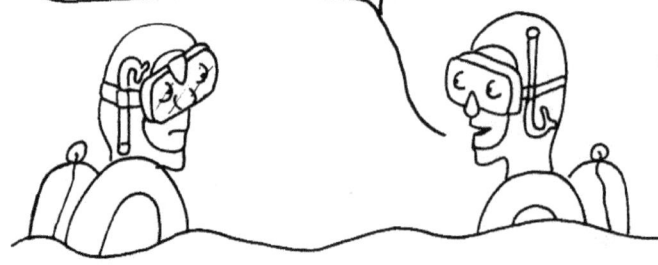

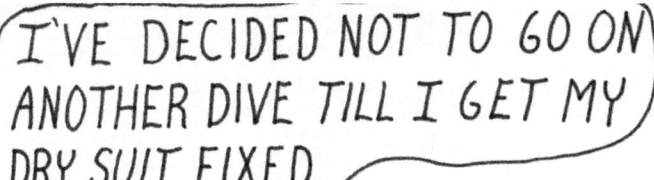
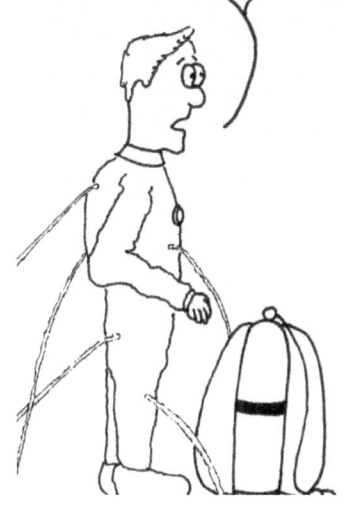
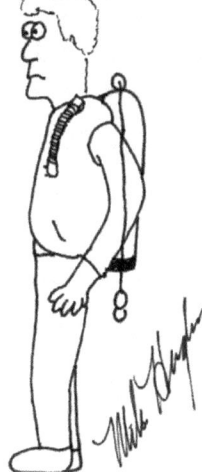

CROSS-SECTIONAL VIEW OF A WOLF EEL DEN

THE ANOYING HABIT OF SEA TURTLES HITCHING RIDES FROM UNSUSPECTING DIVERS

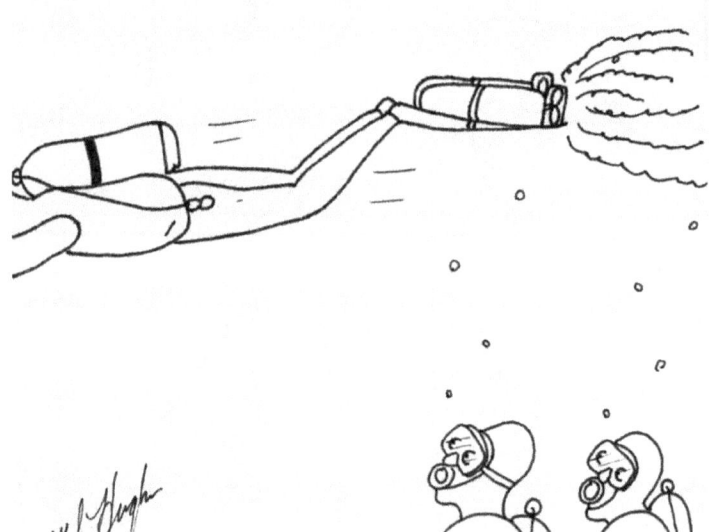
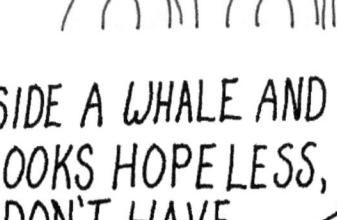

WHOOPS AIRLINES

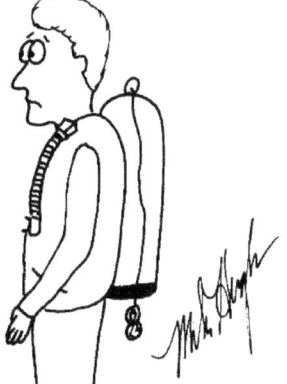

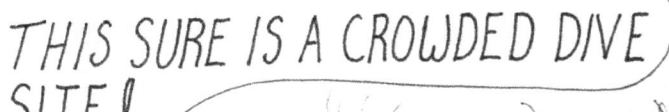

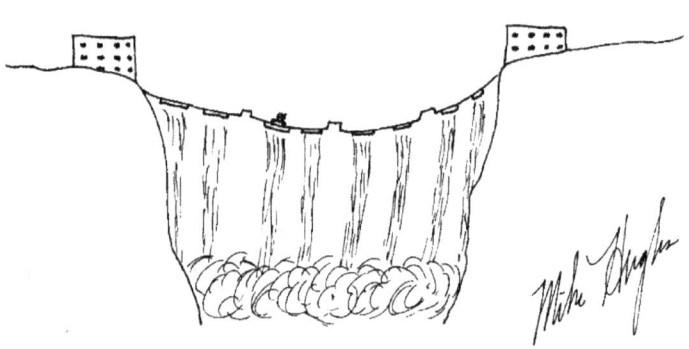

WHOOPS AIRLINES

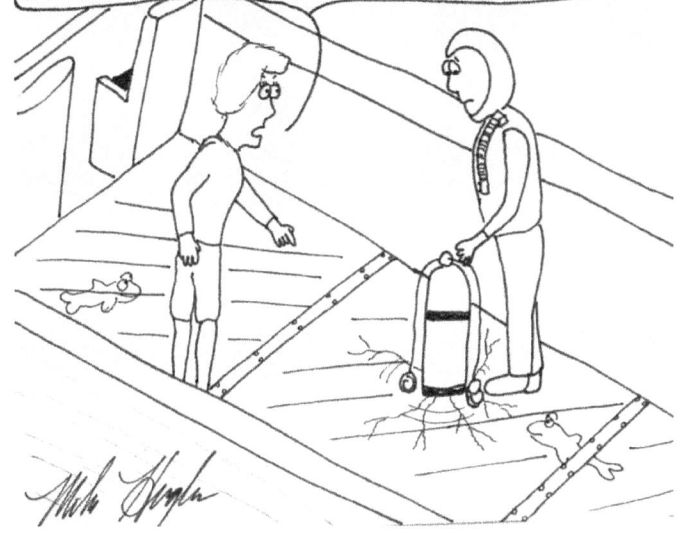

I LIKE DOING UNDERWATER PAINTINGS, BUT I USUALLY RUN OUT OF AIR BEFORE I CAN FINISH THEM.

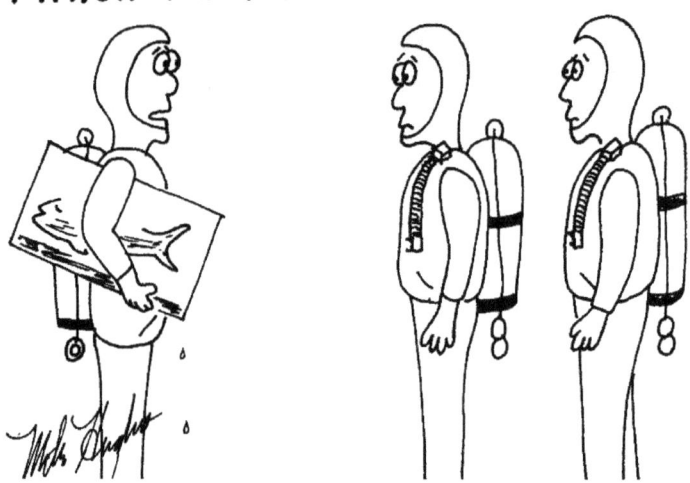

I GOT A CROWN OF THORNS SPINE STUCK IN MY FINGER, BACKED INTO SOME FIRE CORAL, GOT STUNG BY A JELLYFISH, HIT MY HEAD ON THE BOAT... ALL IN ALL, IT WAS A PRETTY GOOD DIVE.

 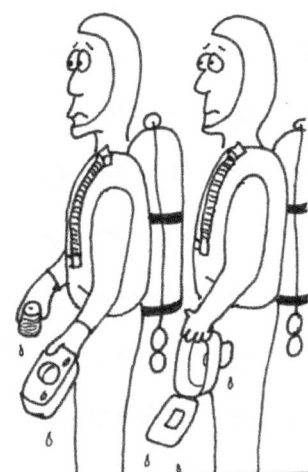

WHOOPS AIRLINES

WHOOPS AIRLINES

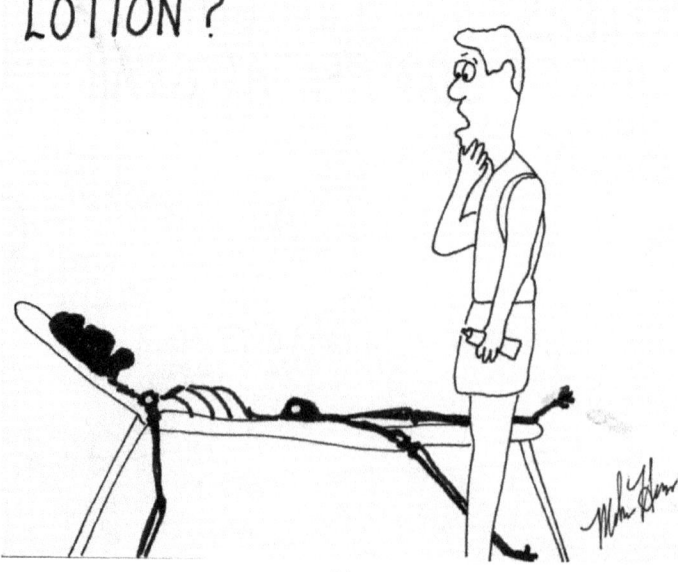

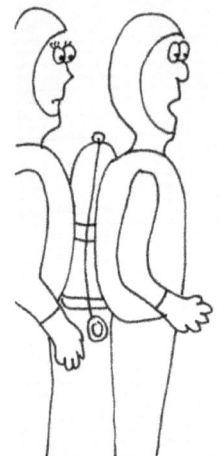
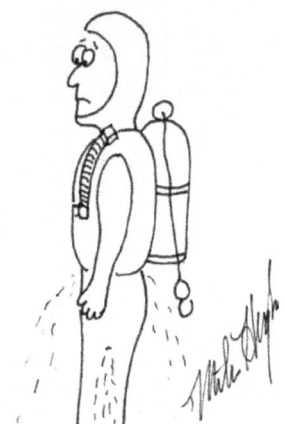

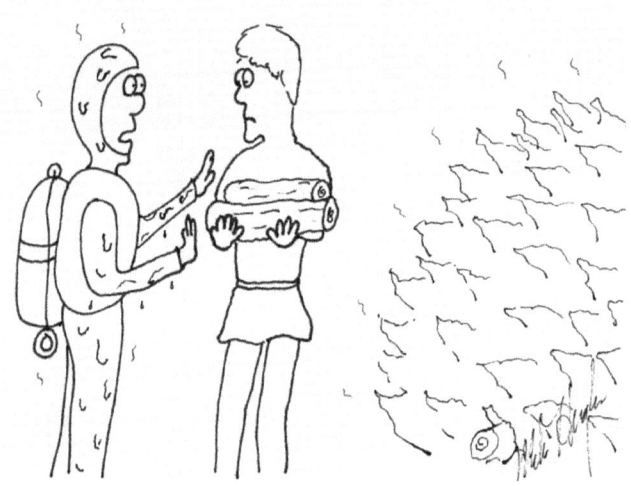

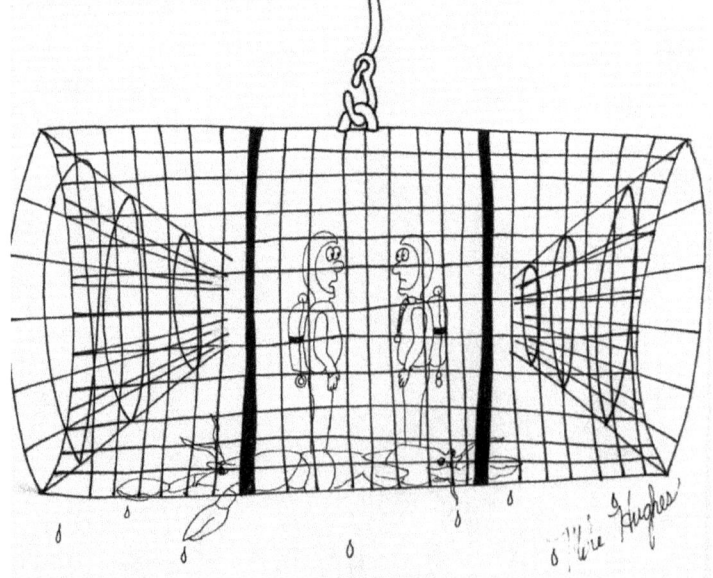

CLOSE ENCOUNTERS!

WHEN I LEFT THE SHOP I HAD 3000 LBS OF AIR IN MY TANK. AFTER THE DIVE I HAD 4000 LBS. DO I GET A REBATE OR SOMETHING?

DURING OUR SAFETY STOP I THOUGHT WE COULD PLAY A GAME. BE CAREFUL THOUGH... SOMETIMES THE PIECES FLOAT AWAY.

FIVE POINT ASCENT:
1. SIGNAL BUDDY O.K. TO ASCEND.
2. CHECK FOR MISSING DIVE WATCH.
3. DETATCH EEL FROM INFLATOR HOSE.
4. WIPE JELLY FISH OFF MASK.
5. SWIM UP OUT OF KELP ENTANGLEMENT.

ICE DIVING / ICE FISHING

NEVER ASCEND AS FAST AS YOUR BUBBLES... UNLESS YOUR TRAPPED INSIDE ONE.

WHOOPS AIRLINES

I CAN'T GO IN THERE... THE FLOOR'S ALL WET.

NEVER KNEW A DIVER COULD JUMP LIKE THAT TIL I HOOKED ONE.

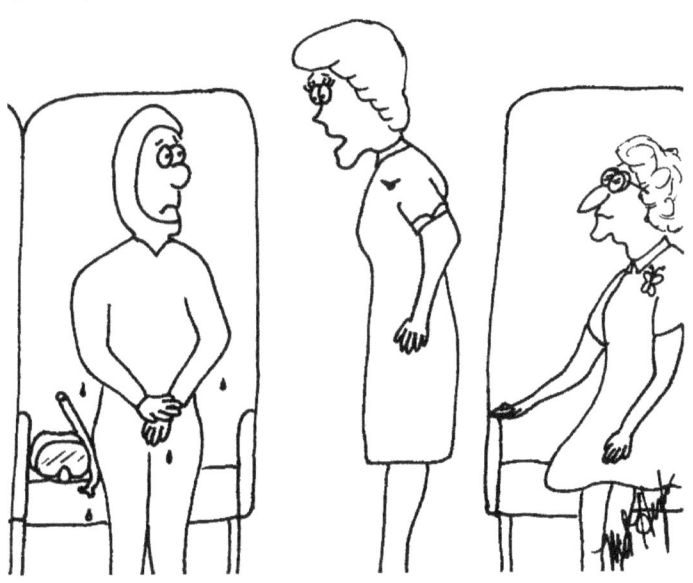

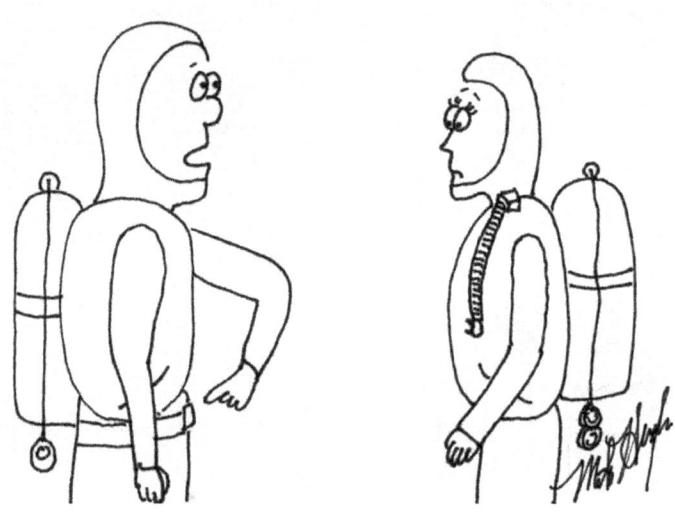

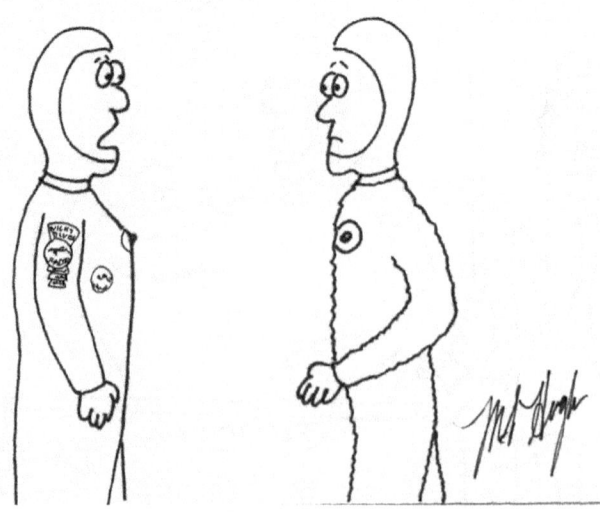

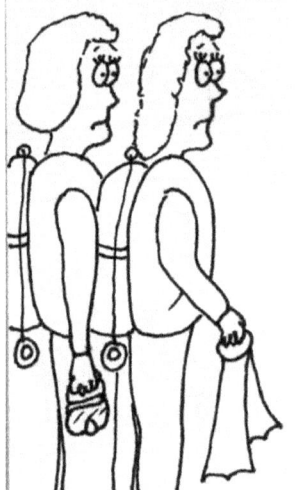

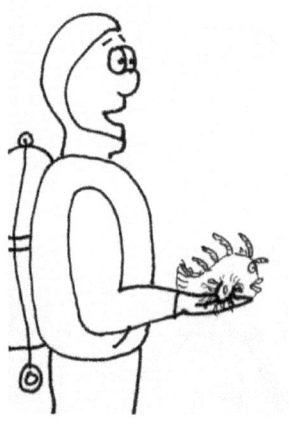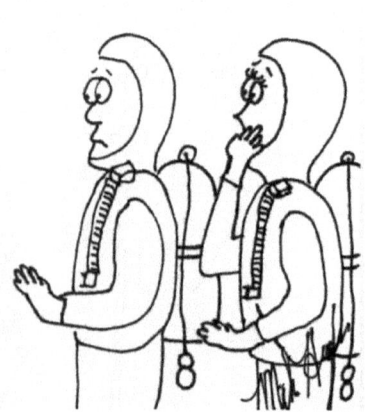

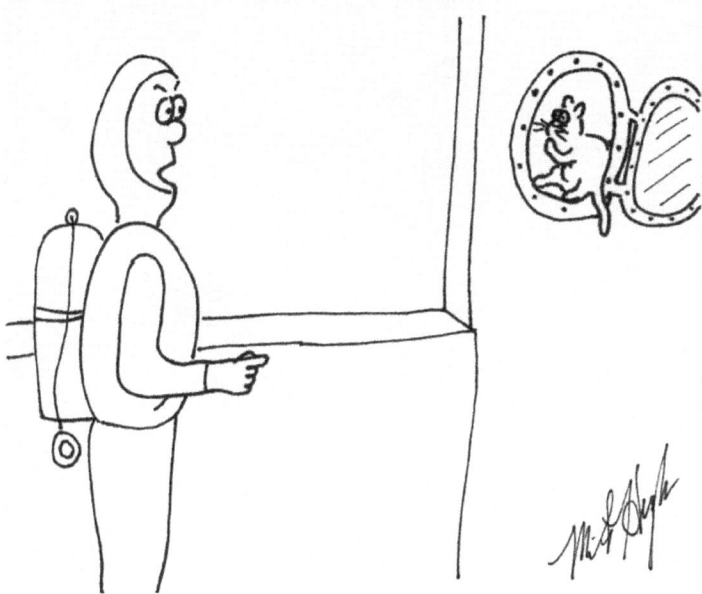

SNORKEL/REGULATOR EXCHANGE: A DEFINITE SURFACE SKILL.

WHOOPS AIRLINES

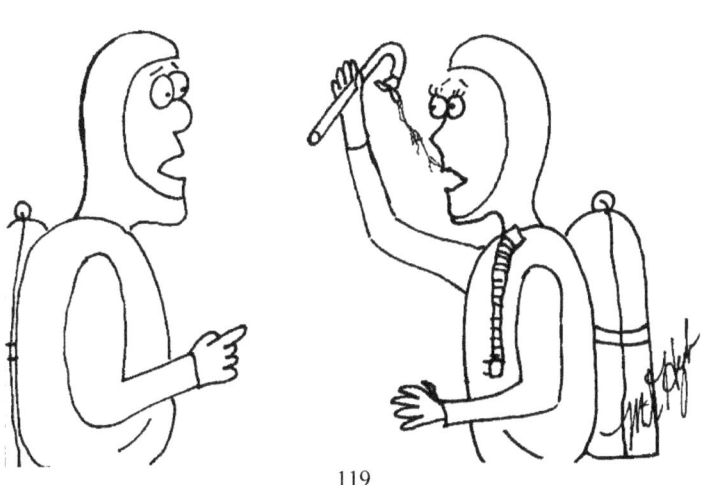

WHOOPS AIRLINES

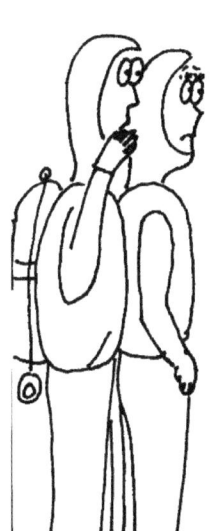
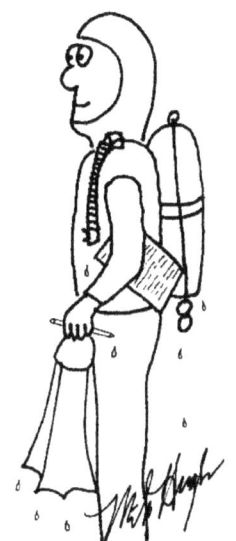

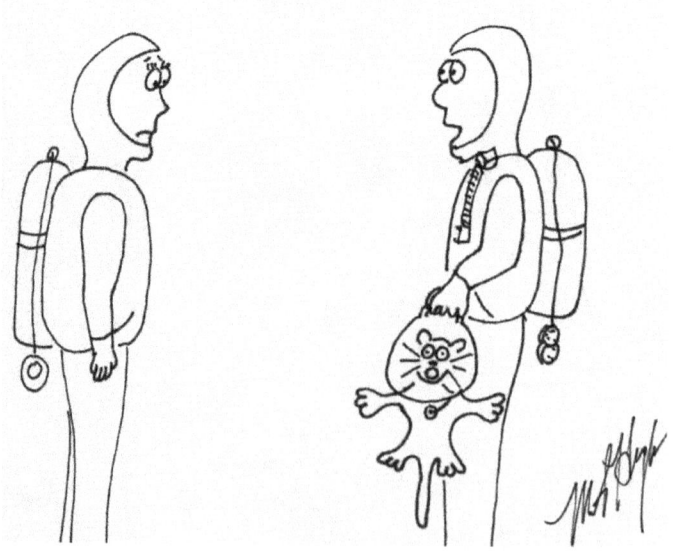

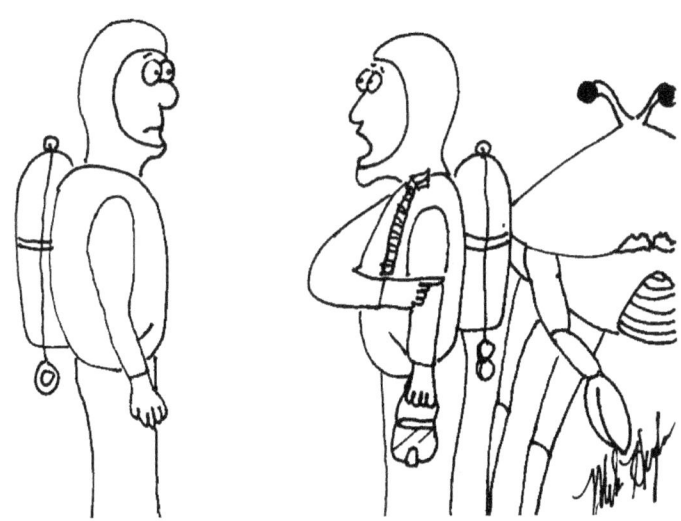

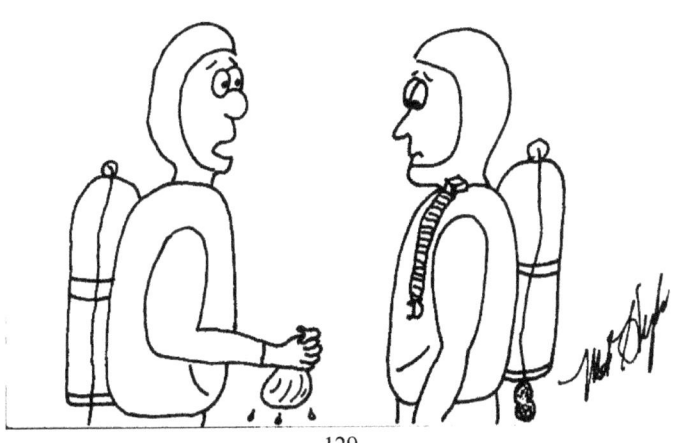

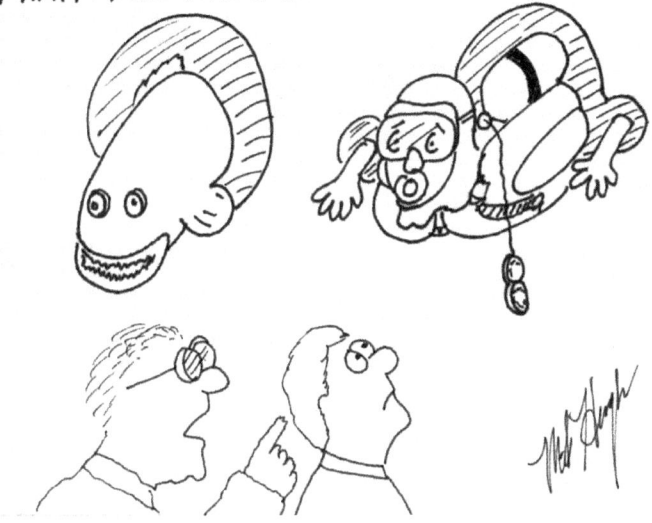

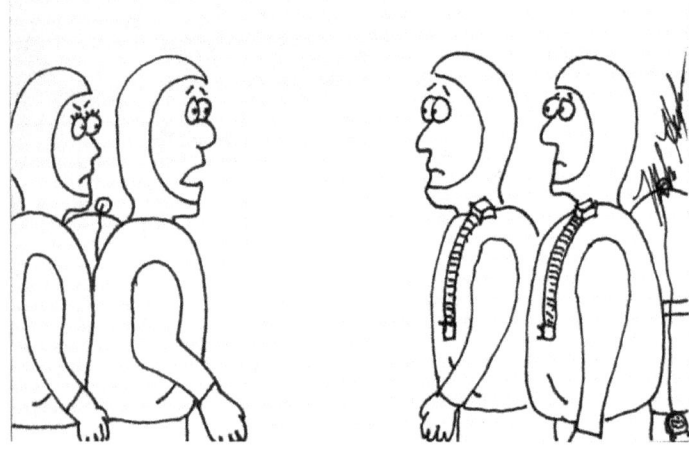

THE JOY OF CAVE DIVING

OH, HE DOESN'T DIVE ANYMORE. ATLEAST NOT AFTER THAT STRANGE ENCOUNTER WITH A LUSTFUL MANATEE.

WHOOPS AIRLINES

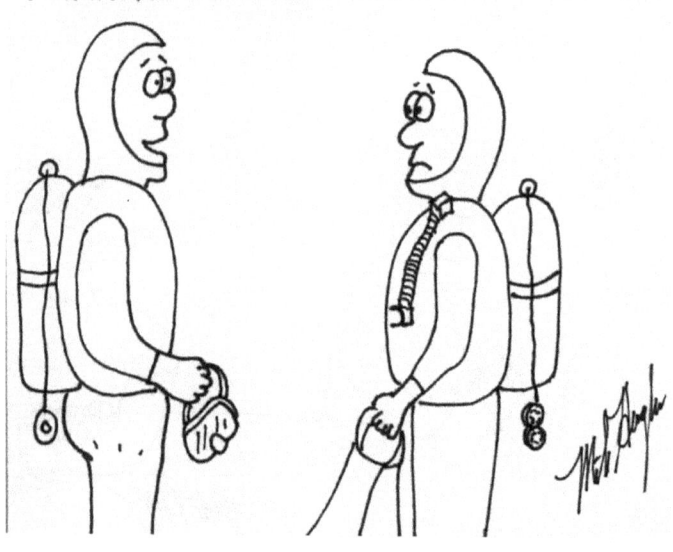

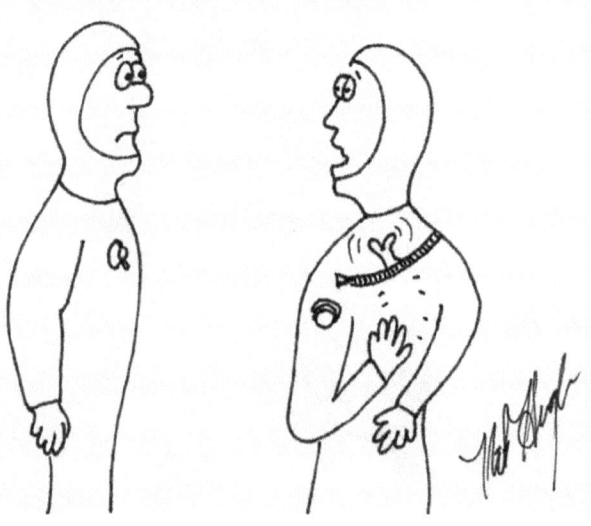

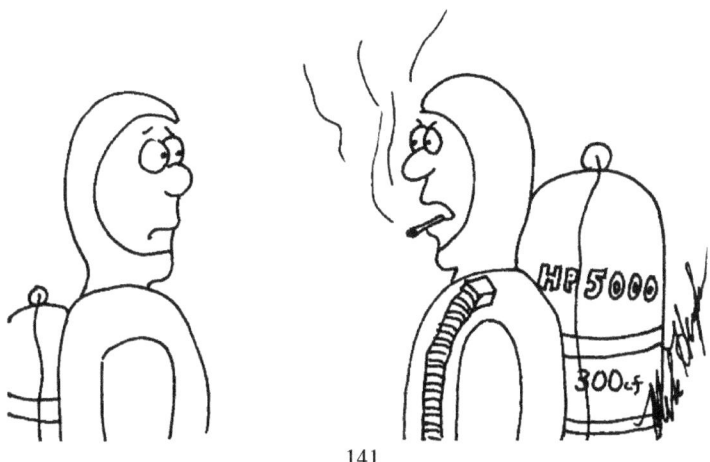

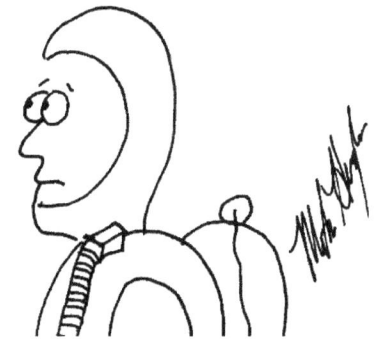

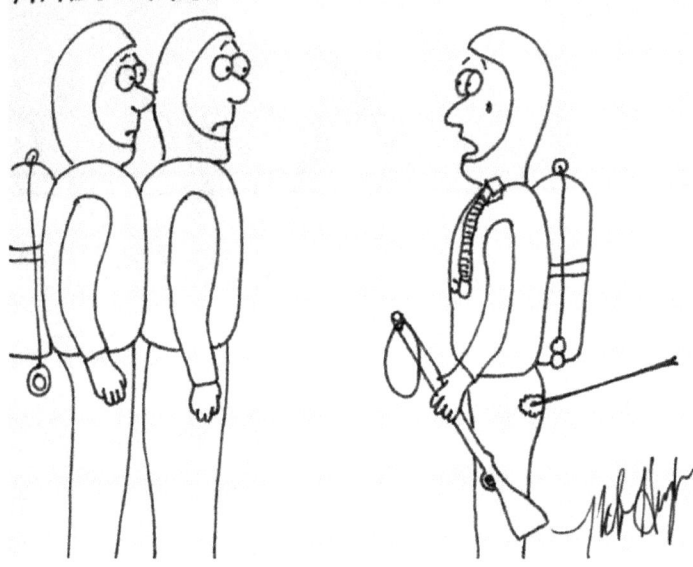

WHOOPS AIRLINES

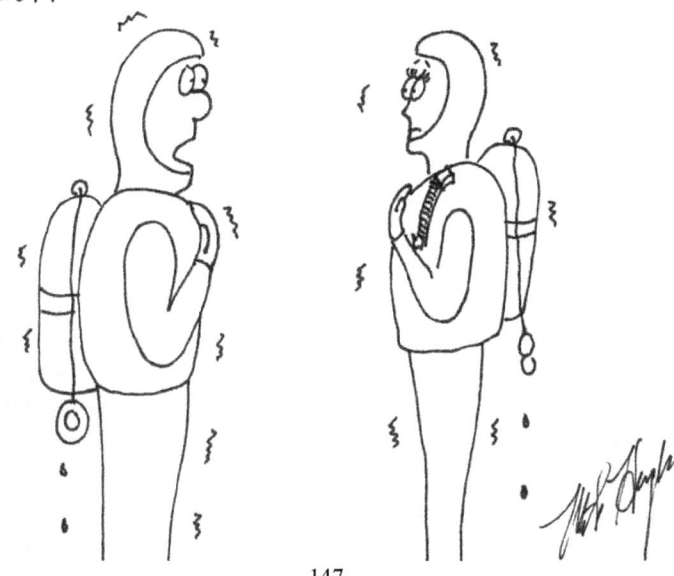

WHOOPS AIRLINES

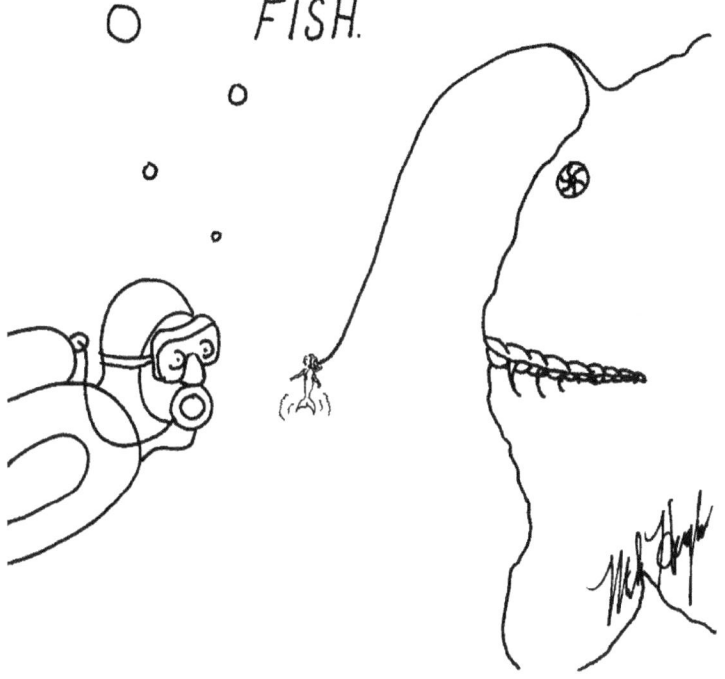

WHOOPS AIRLINES

SEATTLE'S FAMOUS LATTE DIVER

HEY, ARE YOU HAVING MARRIAGE PROBLEMS?... AND BE HONEST.

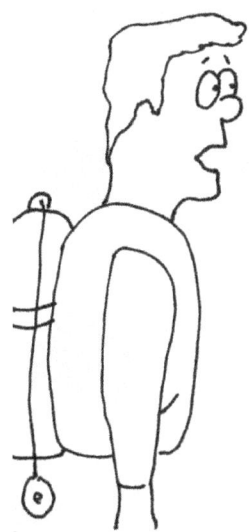 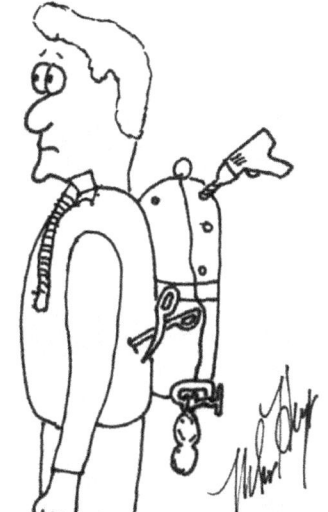

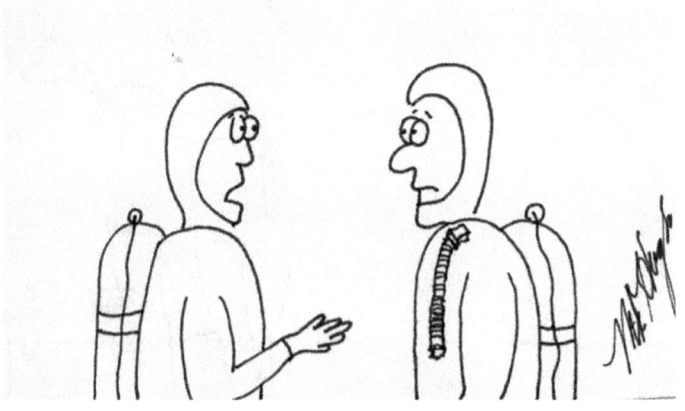

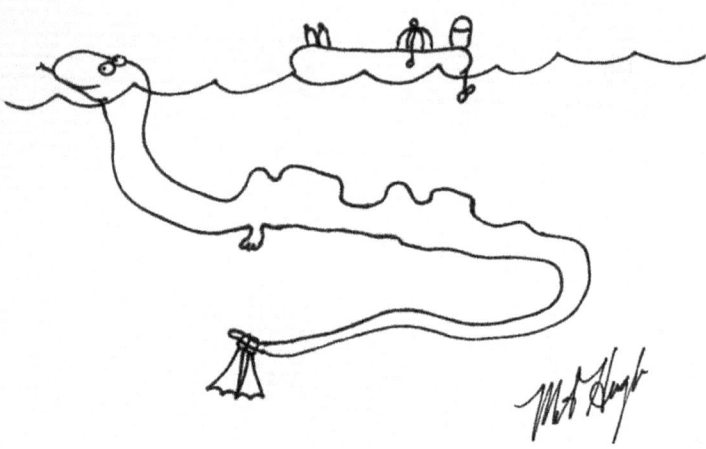

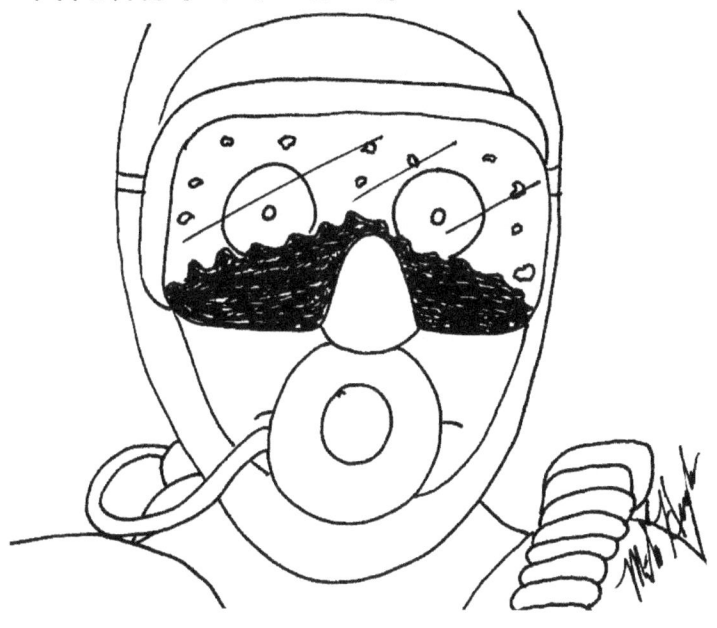

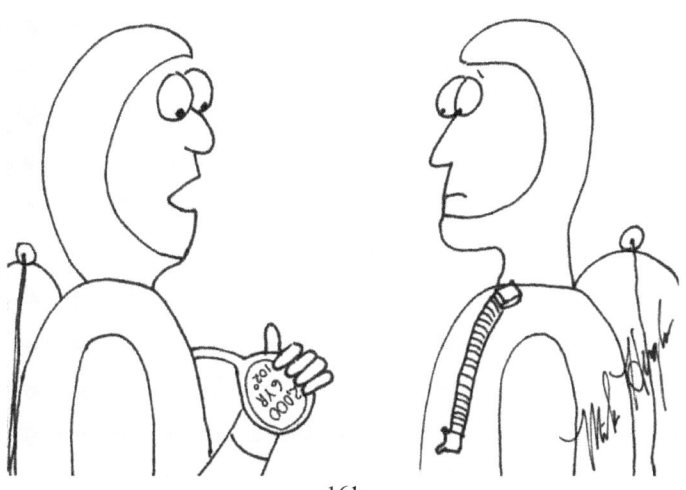

WHOOPS AIRLINES

CAR WASH ONLY PLEASE... THE WAX MAKES ME ITCH.

I KNOW YOU HAVE AN EXTENSIVE DIVING BACKGROUND, BUT DIVING WITH MIXED GASES IS STILL GOING TO BE CHALLENGING FOR BOTH OF YOU.

The New Bottom Timer

BEWARE OF SNORKLE PERCHERS

WHOOPS AIRLINES

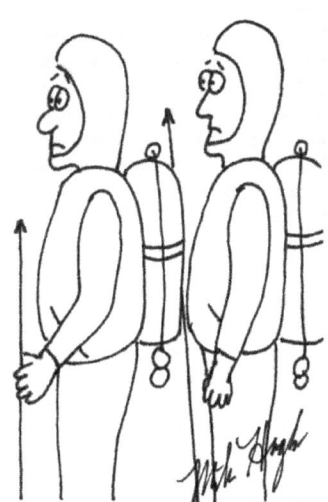

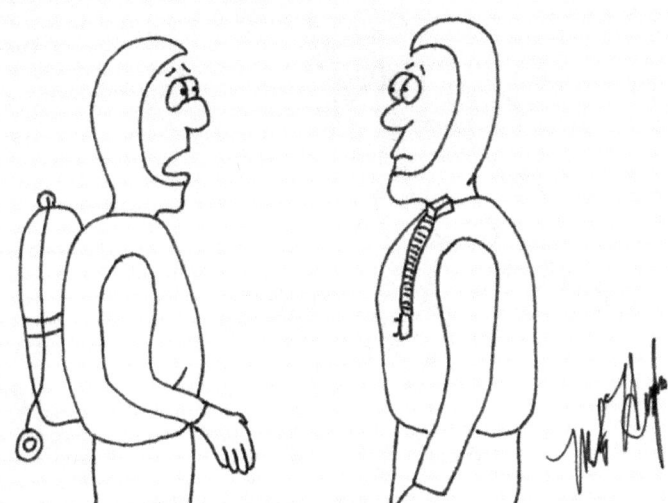

YOU KNOW IT LOOKS BAD TO THE STUDENTS WHEN THE ONLY ONE GETTING KNOCKED OVER BY THE WAVES IS THE INSTRUCTOR.

AND FOR THE SQUEAMISH, FROM NOW ON WE'RE GOING TO SPEAR THE FISH INSTEAD OF BITTING THE FISH BETWEEN THE EYES, CRUSHING THEIR BRAINS, AND KILLING THEM INSTANTANEOUSLY.

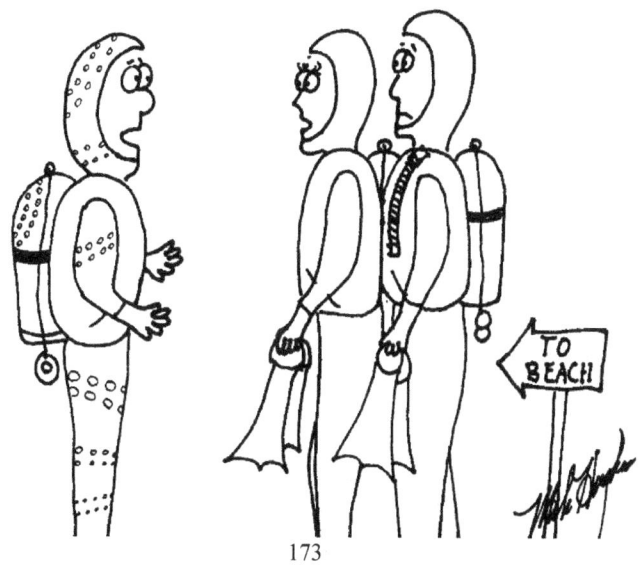

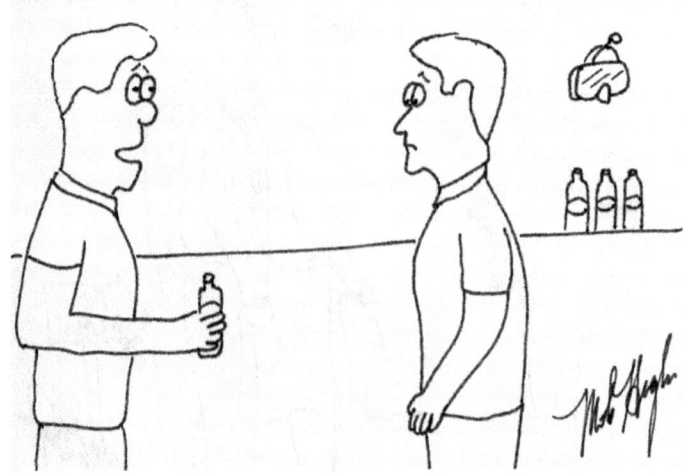

WHOOPS AIRLINES

CAN YOU HELP ME WITH MY FINS?

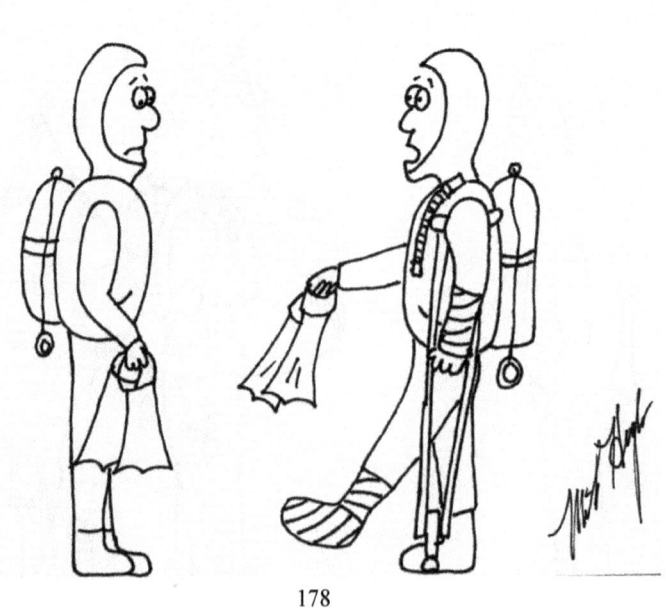

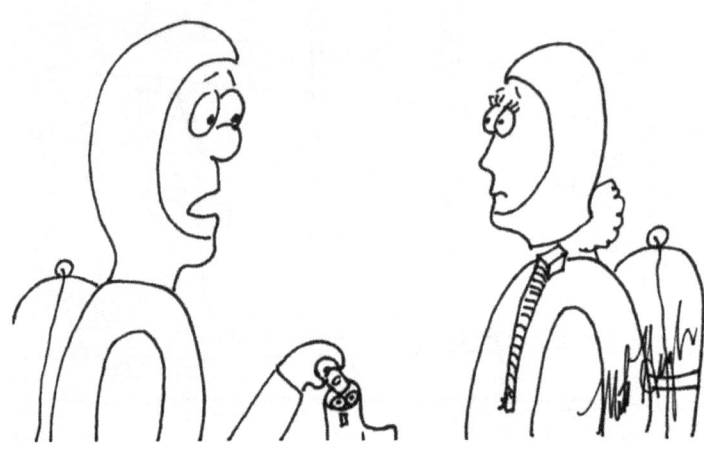

I BLEW A FIN AND SPUN OUT OF CONTROL.

HELLO 911, MY BUDDY AND I ARE STUCK IN THE MUD FLATS. COULD YOU PLEASE SEND A CRANE OR POSSIBLY A HELICOPTER?

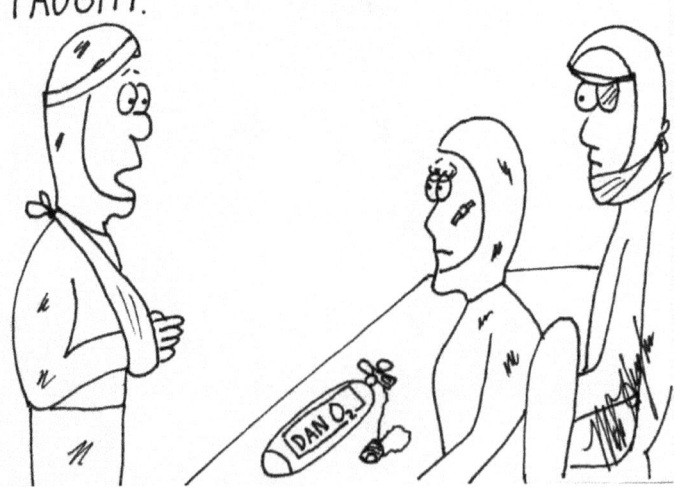

WHOOPS AIRLINES

WHOOPS AIRLINES

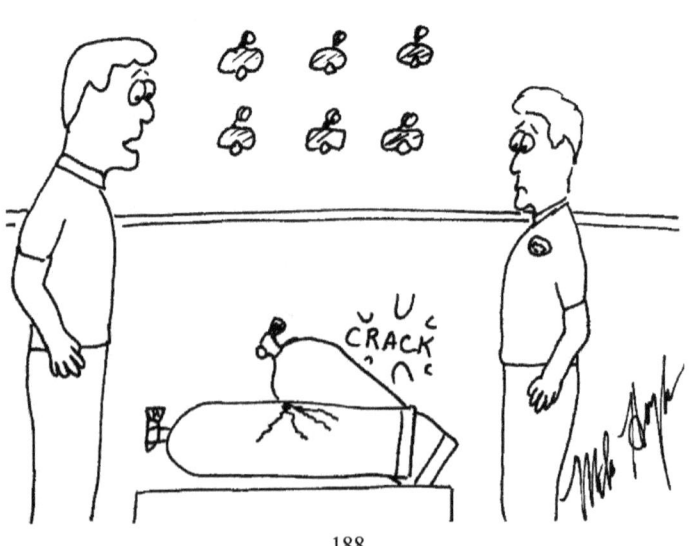

I GOT A RIDE. SEE YA BACK AT SHORE.

TONIGHT WE PARTY TOO MUCH. WITH DEHYDRATION AND A HANGOVER WORKING IN OUR FAVOR, AFTER OUR SHALLOW DIVE TOMORROW, SOME OF US MAY EXPERIENCE A SLIGHT CASE OF THE BENDS. OK, WITH THE DISCLAIMER OUT OF THE WAY, WHO'S READY TO PARTY?

WHOOPS AIRLINES

WHOOPS AIRLINES

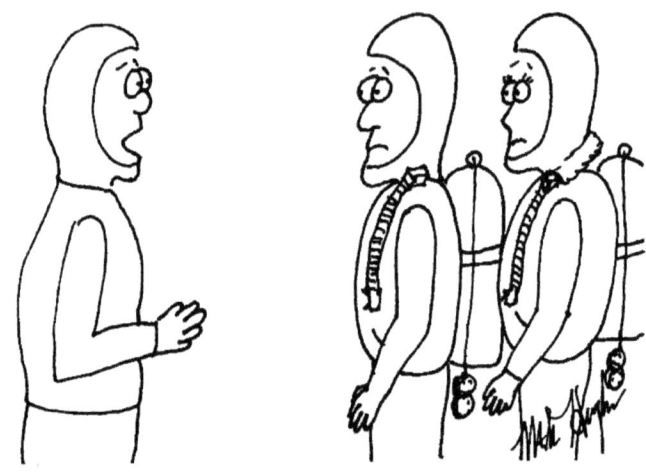

WHOOPS AIRLINES

HE MAY LOOK NORMAL, BUT BELIEVE ME, HE CAN DRINK LIKE A FISH.

CAN YOU FIX THE BACK OF MY WET SUIT? I HAD A GAS LEAK.

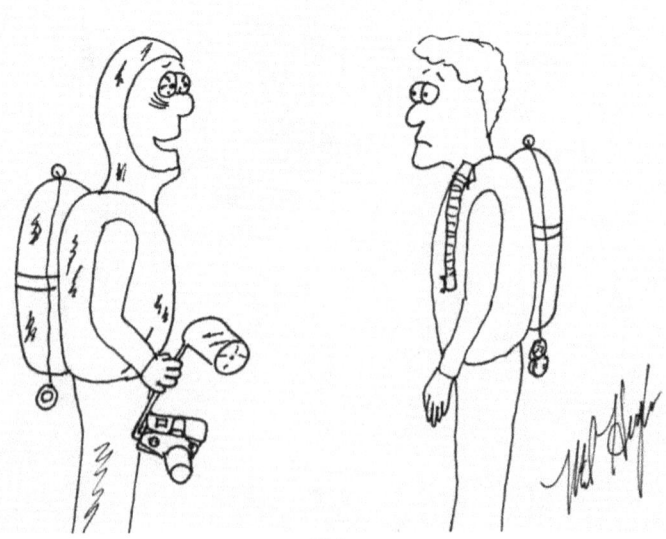

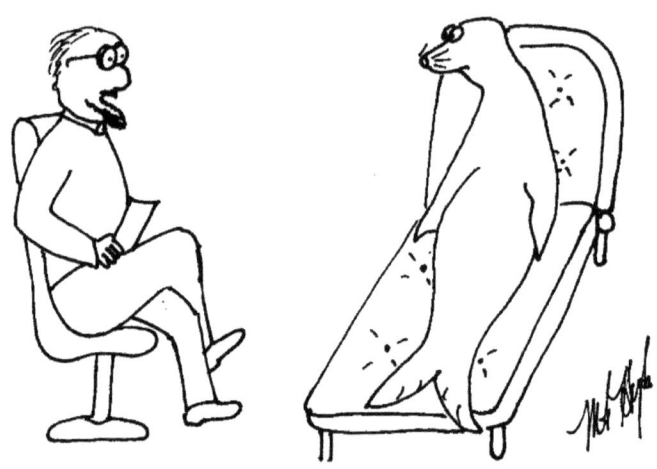

WHOOPS AIRLINES

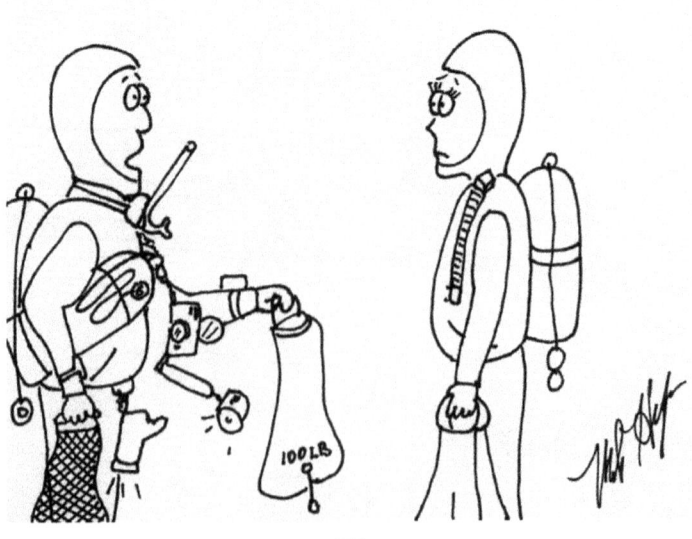

THE END

WHOOPS AIRLINES

www.ingramcontent.com/pod-product-compliance
Lightning Source LLC
Chambersburg PA
CBHW071456040426
42444CB00008B/1359